FOR:

_____

FROM:

_____

MY TWO CENTS:

_____

_____

_____

_____

_____

_____

_____

_____

_____

_____

_____

Two Sense
Practical Wisdom For New Adults

Graduation! The big day is actually, finally here! You are graduating from school, but also into a new chapter of life. Things are different now. You aren't a kid or anyone's dependent any more. Decisions are yours to make. The freedom is amazing and everyone is rooting for you to succeed.

As experienced adults, we remember what it was like to step out into the world for the first time. We fondly recall the way we lived our young lives to the fullest and made choices that would shape the rest of our days. But...we also ran into little life snags – situations that no one spelled out for us. We fumbled our way through, and we definitely had to learn a few lessons the hard way.

But this is the good news! You don't have to make the same mistakes we did. This is our gift to you. We can make your hard knocks a little softer with some practical advice on a handful of common situations which can trip up new adults. Read this booklet, and then focus your energy on living the thrilling and fulfilling life in front of you. Good luck out there, graduate. We are proud of what you have accomplished - but really excited to see what you do next.

AUTHORS:

Jillian Moore Practical wisdom came slowly – she once had her savings split into two accounts because she thought this meant she was earning double interest. Seriously, even smart people can miss some important parts in math class. Her wisdom was earned through trial and error and disaster and success and travel and late nights with great friends. She has previously published a children's book and was a frequent contributor to a Seattle-based satire blog. She has a really nice dog, a super capable dude, and three glorious children.

Tricia Phillips is the holder of a degree in creative writing. As you would expect, this led her to study to be a midwife, spend a year in Prague studying international finance, have a goat farm, and become an executive at large, powerful corporations. But she prefers the mother/writer/farmer roles. She resides in Boise, Idaho.

Other contributors: Cover and interior graphics created by Crossroads Creative.

DISCLAIMER

The authors of this book write these articles from experience, not as financial, legal or any other kind of trained professional. All tips contained herein are purely suggestions for an individual to use along with their own judgement as they navigate the early years of adulthood. Please don't do anything dumb and then claim we told you it was a good idea. Our articles contain things that are good to know and, from our 20/20 hindsight, a good start down the path of not messing up. Also, there is some comedy. So take it with a grain of salt, but know that these are well-intended words from wise people who want you to do well. Also, you can't sue us for anything we say in this booklet.

CONTENTS:

What to do about a bill you can't pay

It happens to everyone. Maybe you broke your arm and had an emergency room visit. The doctor decided that you needed surgery to put a pin in it, and 6 weeks later you are about to get your cast off and get your normal life back. Then it happens. The bills start rolling in. Suddenly you find yourself owing $2,400 because of this thing called a "deductible" for your high deductible insurance plan.

You do not HAVE $2,400. You cannot BORROW $2,400 from your parents or your friends. What do you do?

A. Throw the bills in the garbage immediately and stop collecting the mail

B. Write a Twitter tirade about the messed up medical care and insurance industry and then post a video of you burning the bills

C. Sell your car, your computer, your futon, your turn tables in an attempt to come up with the money

D. Respond to a couple of the credit card offers your get in the mail with the plan to max the new cards out to pay these bills

E. Call the billing department for each bill and tell them you are not able to pay and need to arrange a payment plan

If you selected E, you are CORRECT!! Ignoring the bills will not make them evaporate and will have long-term impact to your credit score (see following chapter, **Why you should care about your credit score**). Selling your car or laptop is just going to make it harder to live your life and earn money to pay future bills.

Before you call the billing departments, you need to figure out what you CAN afford to pay every month. Look at your budget – what's that? You don't have a budget? Okay. I'm not going to get all crazy on you here, but you should have a general idea what you make and what you spend. Put together a simple list like this:

INCOME	**$1,280**
EXPENSES	
Rent (this should not be more than 1/3 your paycheck if at all possible. Get a roommate or two if you must)	**$350**
Phone (shop around for a cheaper plan)	**$80**
Health Insurance	**$200**
Utilities (electricity, gas, water, Wi-Fi – the more roommates you have, the better)	**$30**
Food/Coffee	**$350**
Credit Card Bill (minimum payment – try really hard to not collect credit card debt and if you do, seriously, pay more than the minimum amount. You will never, ever pay it off if you just pay the minimum amount)	**$40**
Transportation (car insurance/gas/parking/transit pass/ Uber/taxi)	**$120**
Savings (try REALLY HARD to budget 5% of your income for a savings account)	**$64**
Total expenses budgeted	**$1,234**
Remainder	**$46**

In this example, you have around $50 a month that you can pay towards these medical bills. Gather up the bills and call the billing department(s).

First, explain that you simply do not have the money to pay these bills in full right now and ask if there are any programs for low income patients which could reduce the total amount due. If there are, prepare for some mailing or scanning or faxing (I know...faxing is archaic but so are hospital billing departments) of income statements, bills, and the like to prove that you really can't pay.

Once the new/revised (or not revised) amount you owe has been determined, you want to set up a payment plan. You can afford to pay $50 a month right now. Most medical centers will work with you to make this possible because they would rather get $2,400 over 4 years than to not get it at all. Also, pay more whenever you can. If you get a raise at work or a bonus or something, pay it on your debt (highest interest debt first). Get out of debt as fast as possible.

You may be thinking, "This sounds like a headache. Why don't I just get a bunch of credit cards and do it that way? I won't have to fax anything and can do it all online or on my phone."

I'll tell you why. 29% interest is why. If you are paying $50 a month on a $2,500 credit card debt, you will end up paying hundreds, if not thousands of dollars more in interest than you would if you went the billing department negotiation route.

The bottom line is, DON'T GIVE UP. A creditor (the person or organization to whom you owe money) USUALLY is reasonable (don't borrow money from unreasonable people. It will not end well. Watch "The Godfather" if you don't believe me) and will work with you if you make an effort. If you try to run from the debt, they will not want to help you and you will be sent to collections which is AWFUL and dehumanizing. Just trust me. Approach the debt with honesty and integrity and a request for help and it should be manageable.

Why you should care about your credit score

A credit score is a three digit number that basically tells banks, potential employers, etc., how likely you are to pay your debts or bail on them/pay them late. For the first couple of years of your life, your credit score may have no impact on your life, but at some point, it will.

Every time you are late with a credit card payment or loan payment or phone payment or utility payment, you run the risk of being reported to the credit bureau. NO ONE WILL TELL YOU that they have reported you to the bureau. If you pay your credit card bill 2 weeks late, you will be charged a fee from the credit card company (often as much as your minimum payment) and the interest rate they charge you will go up (sometimes as much as three times, i.e. from 9.99% interest to 29% interest) AND they will report you to the credit bureaus who calculate your credit score.

A history of on-time payments, using a credit card and paying it on time, the age of your credit card accounts and a record of getting a loan and paying it back as promised, all increases your credit score. Late payments or defaults bring your credit score down. Sometimes WAY down.

But who cares? Right?

- You know that offer to buy a new laptop with "12 months same as cash?" That is a loan, and whether or not you are approved for it depends on your credit score.

- When you apply for a credit card, the interest rate they offer you and the credit line they offer you depends on your credit score.

  » Your first credit card may only give you a $500 limit at first because you don't HAVE a credit history yet. Using this card and paying it off or paying the minimum payment on time (let me take this opportunity to STRONGLY recommend that you pay off your credit card in full every month. Unless there is a real emergency, don't charge stuff that you don't have the money to pay for that month) is what builds up your credit history and credit score

- You decide to buy a 3 year old car and there is a great offer for a loan with 0% interest for the first 12 months. Your credit score determines whether you can get a loan to buy that car (also see, ***Intro to intelligent car buying, page 19***)

  » Also, if you DO get that loan but the first month the payment sneaks up on you and you haven't set up auto-pay yet and it is a day late, guess what? You don't have a 0% interest loan anymore. You might have a 20% interest loan now and your total cost for that car has gone way up.

- EMPLOYERS sometimes will run a credit report on you to determine how risky you are as an employee. Do you have a history of running out on your responsibilities? Are you in serious financial trouble and maybe working with large amounts of cash or expensive goods would be too tempting for you? This can influence the hiring decision for some jobs. You can think this is unfair, but that won't change it.

- Someday, you might decide to buy a condo or a house and need a loan. A good credit score versus a bad one can determine whether or not you can get a loan, and how much you will pay in interest over the life of the loan:

» A $200,000 loan paid over 30 years at 3.5% interest will actually cost you around $320K

» A $200,000 loan paid over 30 years at 6.5% interest will actually cost you around $450K

If you are buying a condo or home with a partner, and they qualify for a good rate but you qualify for a bad rate, your home loan will be the bad rate and your partner will probably be kind of pissed off for the life of that loan.

It takes a long time to fix a bad credit report. If you are already in trouble, there are some great organizations to help you but there are also some scams intended to fleece desperate people. If you do want help creating a plan to get and stay out of debt, look for credit counselors approved by the Federal Trade Commission and U.S. Department of Justice.

The point is, START NOW to have a good credit score. It isn't complicated – just pay your bills on time and if you can't pay them, call the creditor to figure out what you CAN do (see previous article, *What to do about a bill you can't pay*). It seems like some far-away thing that doesn't matter or some crazy conspiracy laden voodoo, and an argument can be made for that, but your credit score will have a tangible impact on your life someday, so take care of it. Also, go to the dentist for your regular cleanings. You will thank me for both of these things when you are 45.

You can get a truly free credit report once a year. There are lots of companies who offer you a free credit report and then trick you into paying for other things. Go to www.annualcreditreport. com which is the ONLY FTC approved annual free credit report website.

What to do if a friend wants to borrow money

Borrowing and loaning money can screw up a friendship faster than you can say "resentment." Let's say you loan your friend $100 to make rent. Let's say you aren't rolling in money and it is kind of hard for you to part with that money. It means eating ramen more than you would like in the coming two weeks and drip coffee made AT HOME (LIKE A CAVEMAN!), but this person is your friend and they are on the cusp of eviction, so it feels really good to help them out, and it makes you not even MIND the ramen and drip coffee (MADE AT HOME. LIKE A CAVEMAN).

Yes, you feel really good about yourself and your generosity until you see your friend on the corner holding a $7 Frappuccino with an Anthropologie bag on their arm, and I don't care how good the sale was, you are probably going to be angry.

Or you find out that the friend has developed a drug problem and they lied to you about what they were going to use the money for.

Or the friend has a deadbeat boyfriend who lives in her apartment but quit his job because they wanted him to start his shift at 7am and that "isn't how he rolls" so he isn't contributing to their rent or any other expenses and you realize that you are supporting HIM. Suddenly you feel entitled to have a very strong opinion about how fast she should dump this loser and it creates instant friction. Now you are acting like her parent instead of her friend, and that sucks for both of you.

These scenarios do not make for a stronger friendship. These scenarios are likely to ruin a friendship much faster than if you had said, "No, I'm sorry. I can't spare the money right now. I hope it works out. I'll keep my eyes open for any extra work for you." (See, ***How to make a little bit of quick money in a way that you won't regret forever, page 15.***)

You may be thinking, "Dude, this is really harsh, and ungenerous and that isn't how I ROLL." But I'm not finished yet.

I DO loan money to friends, except secretly, I don't think of it as a loan. When someone asks me for money, I ask myself, "Would I be okay giving them this money for whatever they need it for, and never getting that money back? Would I be able to meet MY financial obligations, would I be able to still love this friend even if I gave them $100 and they used it in a different way than I would (on a new pair of shoes or a 90 minute massage) and I never saw it again?" If the answer is yes, then I loan them the money. I do not TELL them that I don't expect to see the money again, and there is still a spoken expectation that they pay me back, but in my head and my heart and my wallet, I am not counting on it. If and when they DO pay me back (and like 75% of the time they do) it is a lovely surprise. If they DON'T pay me back, it doesn't bother me, and if it DOES bother me, I take responsibility for making the wrong decision in giving them that money. Next time I'll probably make a different decision. I think of it like a "Go Fund Me" donation. The money was asked for, I decided to give it and I expect nothing in return. This is easier when a friend is borrowing $20 than when they are borrowing $500, but I've had good luck applying the premise in both situations.

The other, more traditional option would be to ask the friend who wants to borrow money when they expect to pay it back, and then WRITE IT DOWN. It doesn't have to be formal or anything. Create a note on your phone using your notepad app and create a calendar reminder for a couple of days after they said they would get the money back to you and on that day, if they HAVEN'T paid you back, send them a text saying, "Hey—how is it going? I wondered if you were going to be able to pay me back that $50 this week?" and then they do or they don't or they come up with a reason that they can only give you $10 this week and they PROMISE they will pay the rest in 2 weeks on their next paycheck. And then you update the note on your phone.

You can totally do it that way, but don't blame me if you end up resentful and it changes the dynamics of the friendship.

Also, on the flip side, if you find yourself needing to borrow money from a friend, BE CONSERVATIVE about what you say regarding when you can pay it back. If you think you MIGHT be able to pay it back on the next paycheck, don't promise that. Promise that you can pay half of it back on the next paycheck and half on the following. Make promises that you can keep, not promises that you think will make your friend say yes, and which you WANT to keep but in reality probably can't. This is true in a million situations. In the business world, they call it "under-promise and over-deliver" but you don't have to call it that. You can just call it, "don't promise the best case scenario—promise the most realistic scenario and then surprise people if/when you do better than that!"

DO NOT, I repeat, DO NOT, assume that the person from whom you are borrowing is using the "this loan is really a gift and what a lovely surprise if I see that money again" mentality. They almost certainly are not. They are probably using the "Did they buy a new shirt with the money I loaned them??? WHEN WILL I GET MY MONEY BACK??" mentality, so borrow and pay back money accordingly. And always pay it back. ALWAYS. That phone notepad app and calendar thing works both ways. Write it DOWN when you borrow money and hold yourself accountable so your friends and family don't have to.

The magic of compound interest

Money tends to run through your fingers like water when you are first out on your own. There are just so many things to want, especially when your dreams of travel or a full back tattoo are within reach. However, just for a moment, envision what NOT spending your money NOW can do for your bank account LATER. I know, retirement is so far away, it's hard to get motivated. But if your goal is to one day become a multi-millionaire – planting one magic bean can actually bring that closer to reality. That bean is called compound interest.

Compound interest is interest calculated on the initial investment and also on the accumulated interest of previous periods. Think of it as getting interest on your interest. It makes your investment grow exponentially more than it would in a simple interest situation. The earlier you start socking money away, the more interest it gains, and the more interest on that interest you gain.

Dig: Let's say you can scrape together $1000 annually (that's less than $40 each bi-monthly paycheck) and put into an account bearing 3% monthly compound interest. In 30 years, having invested 30k, you will now have over 48k, a handsome profit of 18k on your money.

If you wait 15 years, but begin investing $2000 annually in the same 3% compound interest account, the same investment of 30k only has time to accumulate 8k in interest. You have paid in the same amount but earned 10k less.

Starting Saving at 25 vs. 35

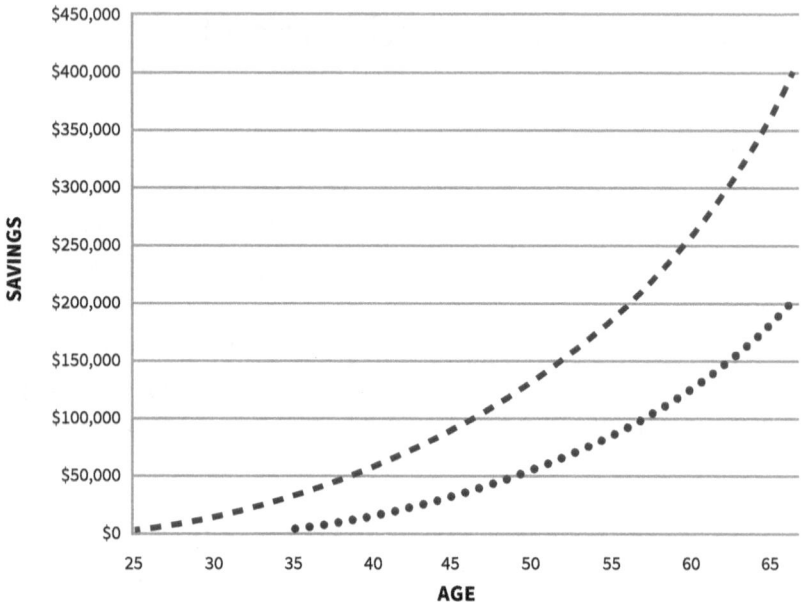

In the investing world, time really is money. Waiting until you are older to start saving means you will have to contribute much more to get the same return.

How to make a little quick money in ways that you won't regret forever

It happens to everyone. Your cat gets sick and you have to pay $250 at the vet or YOU get sick and you miss two shifts at work, or you go on a mini-road trip with your friends and somehow end up spending $200 on food and your share of gas and hotel room when you had estimated $50. Suddenly you do the math and realize that you are not going to be able to make rent in a week or pay your phone bill. Do you:

A. Call your parents and beg for money and prepare for a lecture about how they told you that having a pet was a big responsibility and that you couldn't afford it, or that you should be taking your vitamins and eating more kale so you don't get sick or that maybe NOW you realize how much money it costs to have a vacation and maybe NOW you can appreciate the trips you were taken on and why you couldn't have a souvenir everywhere we stopped.

B. Ask your friends with the best paying jobs or most generous parents if you can borrow some money. (See, *What to do if a friend asks to borrow money, page 9.*)

C. Sell your plasma (blood, not television), try to get odd jobs and sell books and clothes that you legitimately don't want anymore

D. Go to a pawn shop and pawn your grandmother's ring or your grandfather's watch – you'll get it back in a month when you've gotten caught up after all! Probably…

E. Find a local drug study that is looking for healthy non-smokers between age 18 and 30 to participate in a two week double blind medication study for sleep aids

The answer is C! EARN THAT MONEY in a way that will not cause lasting damage to your body, relationships, self-respect or connection to the past.

The amount that you can earn for a plasma donation depends on the current needs, but the highest paying plasma companies pay anywhere from $ 20 - $ 50 per donation, and you can give twice a week, assuming you don't have any health issues that prevent you from doing so. You are helping to save lives AND making a little change. Win/Win. And unlike other "bodily fluid donation for pay" offers, you can tell your parents about this one and also not worry about any surprises showing up in 20 years as a result of this choice.

If bloodletting isn't your jam, reach out to your social network (and the social network of your parents, teachers, bosses, etc.) and offer your services as babysitter, house/pet sitter, dog walker, tutor, house cleaner, lawn mower/weed puller, chanteuse, or whatever other tasks you can think to do. Before you do this, make sure you are qualified to do the work that you are offering to do. If you are allergic to grass and have never mowed a lawn, don't offer to do yardwork. If little kids really annoy you, for the love of all that is holy, don't try to get a babysitting gig!

Figure out what you can competently offer, and then figure out how much the going rate is. Independent house cleaners charge $15-25 an hour depending on where you live and how good you are. House-sitters and pet sitters can get $20-50 a day depending on how much work there is (is there a healthy cat to feed twice a day or three dogs and two cats and half of them have special medical conditions that require creams and pills?

The price should change dramatically in those situations). Baby-sitting is apparently $10-20 an hour depending on whether you are expected to drive the kids, feed the kids, if there is an infant, and where you live.

The important thing here is to know what you deserve to earn for the work and ask for it. Don't do the old, "Oh, whatever you want to pay me is fine" thing when someone asks you what you charge for a service. It is uncomfortable for the person hiring you and for you. Own your worth, and ask for it. Also, do a really good job, not because you want to make a career of pet-sitting or housecleaning, but because you never know when you might need an extra $50 towards the next mini-road trip, vet bill or sick day slush fund.

Intro to intelligent car buying

So you want to buy a car. Before you do, pause and reflect; do you REALLY need a car? If you live in a major metropolitan area with a great transit system, challenge yourself to use it for a year before you bow to the convenience of a car. Hear me out—I know it is part of the American dream and everything, but cars are EX-PENSIVE!

Not only will you pay for the car, but you'll also be shelling out monthly for insurance. If you take out a loan to purchase the car, that means collision AND liability insurance will be required (which is a lot more money). You will need gas (or electricity if you go with a car running on alternative energy), oil changes (unless you go alternative energy!) and new tires, which always cost way more than you expect.

You will get parking tickets and the occasional speeding ticket; it happens to the best of us. There will be annual fees for licensing and emission checks. Then there are the serious break downs that will call for a new transmission or alternator. A car can be extremely financially draining, so if there is a way to do without one, TRY.

If you decide that you really, truly do need a car, if it is at all possible, save money and buy a car with cash. You may not be able to afford the vehicle of your dreams, but you WILL be able to afford something serviceable and enjoy some walking around money instead of a loan payment. You can trick your sensible sedan out with decals and cha-cha balls, cover it in political bumper stickers, dent it in a parking garage without feeling badly

- it's paid for! Remember, cars don't appreciate, they depreciate. Your ride is not an investment. Being car-poor doesn't make a lot of sense unless you are a devoted gearhead or someone who values the perception of status.

Buying a car has changed. Not very long ago it meant matching wits with a salesman and his faceless manager upstairs, who would good cop/bad cop you into overpaying for the car you had fallen in love with on a TV commercial. It was a laborious negotiation process, especially for the buyer who had almost no information at their fingertips – but those days are gone! Now there are just a few simple steps between you and the car of your sensible, fuel efficient dreams.

1. There is no sexy way to put this: if you don't have cash, the smart thing to do is to get prequalified for a car loan. It's the only way for you to realistically know what price range to look in. Banks generally like to finance cars less than five years old, as they have lower miles and are often still under warranty. Look for the lowest APR you can find from a reputable bank and get clear on the purchase criteria. They will furnish you with a letter and you will know that it is finally time to...

2. Do your internet research! Do not, repeat, DO NOT stop by any car dealerships on the way home, even with your pre-qualification letter in hand. No test drives for you, not yet. Instead, take some time and go to a reputable website (True-car.com or Edmonds.com are two commonly used) that can help you narrow down your search within your price range. Figure out what model, year, and mileage you can afford. Are there amenities you can't live without? Or those that you can give up? Target a couple of cars that meet your criteria and your style and are in your price range. See what they are selling for around your area. Print out pages and keep them

Do not let the word "Certified" convince you to skip doing the right research. Many 90 day warranties offered with certified cars only cover the power train. Look for the Buyers Guide on the window – a federally mandated disclosure about the vehicle's warranty. If the salesperson says the car has a warranty but the Buyers Guide sticker says "As Is," the sticker overrides the salesperson.

for reference as you search. Now you know how much the car you want to buy is going for and you have an artifact to consult if you ever become tempted to buy something that is outside your budget or doesn't fit your needs. You know what your car should cost and now GO GET YOUR CAR!

3. Wait. One more little thing. Do you have insurance? You won't be able to test drive a car or purchase one off the lot without collision insurance. So, get that if you don't have it. If you have insurance on a different car, that's good enough for now. Note that your insurance may go up with an upgraded car, you can call ahead to run the numbers. NOW go get your car.

4. The first hour of car shopping is always pretty fun. You sit in cars, you drive them around, you exclaim over seat warmers. The salesperson will be close, but don't pay them any mind because you already know what the car is worth. DO point out any flaws you find in the vehicle that might figure into the price you offer on the car. Don't be rude, but don't let anyone rush you through the process of assessing the car.

» Test Drives: Take your potential car on both side roads and a highway. Listen for ugly sounds like grinding or rattling. It's a good idea to bring your most critical friend, the one who finds fault in everything, with you. Make sure the interior of the car is comfortable and functional. Do

Bad Times For Car Buying

Good Times For Car Buying

DECEMBER
Especially the end

LATE FALL
Newest models on the market

LATE SUMMER
Inventories are being reduced

AFTER NEW YEAR
Sales trend up in first months of year

EARLY FALL
Making room for new models

all the seat belts and windows work? How about the heat and the A/C? Try not to get emotionally attached when you see the Wi-Fi integrated dash and back-up camera. Check the miles – 12k per year is average. Higher miles usually mean a lower price. A car nearing 80k miles might be getting ready for some costly routine maintenance.

5. You think you like the car! It seems like a sweet deal. But wait, just a little more research stands between you and a great decision - get the VIN! The Vehicle Identification Number keeps a mechanical record of the car through multiple

owners. By doing a little web research you can make sure your sweet baby hasn't been in a flood or a rebuild crash. If the seller is at all weird about giving the VIN to you, assume the worst. If they offer it freely and it matches all over the car, run the report. The seller might also offer to run it for you or have it on file. Think long and hard about purchasing a car with a dark past. You can't heal it with your care and love. Or at least, not cheaply. Little things tend to go perpetually wrong with previously damaged cars. You do not need that. If something doesn't check out, be prepared to walk away. There are ALWAYS new cars coming onto the market. Try again tomorrow.

6. If all indicators are that you have found the right car for you, begin negotiation with the salesperson. This part is EASY. Tell them what you believe to be the fair price for the car. Don't low-ball to the extent that it's ridiculous. Offer on the low end of the average price range. Tell them you are pre-qualified and can buy it NOW if they say yes. Don't get into any sort of "Well, what do you need your payments to be?" conversation. The car is worth what it is worth based on market value. The salesperson will counter and you will evaluate based on what you know the car is worth. Only accept an offer that you know to be a fair price. Stick to your guns, know your top price, and be prepared to walk away. They may let you. They may call you in a week to say they have reconsidered. They may NEVER call, but all this time the power is yours because you know what the car has been selling for and will not be taken advantage of. Begin looking for another car to fit your requirements if the first doesn't work out.

A brief word on buying your car from an owner directly. Never, ever take delivery of a car without the title. The person selling the car must match the person ON the title, check their ID. If they don't match, they can't sell you the car. The seller will sign the back of the title, fill out mileage, and the selling price. Now the onus is on you to transfer the title at the DMV. You will have to pay a licensing fee and registration fee. Check the laws in your state as in some states it is a criminal offense not to transfer the title within a certain number of days, but it is good practice to register the car very soon after purchase to avoid confusing liability issues in case of an accident. Make sure you are prepared to pay sales tax on the purchase amount for the car when you register it. It is tempting to write in a lower amount that what the car is worth – but this may bring you to the attention to the IRS. Swath yourself in an IRS cloak of invisibility by paying tax on your purchase.

Dealer or Owner?

Some people would NEVER buy from a dealer because they are positive that they will be pressured and end up overpaying. Some people would NEVER buy from an individual because they are afraid of getting scammed. If you do the research outlined above and feel confident in your ability to walk away if anything feels weird (and for the love of god, always take someone with you if you are going to check out a car you found on Craigslist) you should be able to get a good deal in either place. Buying a car from a friend of the family is also a great option because they are the least likely to sell you something that has secret problems.

How to make a roommate contract and other renting tips

Your first apartment! It's kind of small and has a partial view of the old bowling alley, but it's yours and you are STOKED. Well, yours and Steve's. Steve works at the same place as you and is also moving out of his folk's house. You don't know him that well, but he seems cool and at least you know he gets a regular paycheck. You sign a short lease – six months – to make sure you and Steve get along well before getting into something long term.

The two of you scrape together money for the damage deposit and first/last month's rent. You had no idea moving into a new place would cost triple the monthly rent. So now your bank account is basically empty. But you don't mind subsisting on ketchup packets for a few weeks, you have your own place at last!

Typical Move-In Costs

- 1st month's rent $1,000
- Security deposit $1,000 (often about 1 months' rent, which you may recoup later)
- Moving costs $20 – 500, depending on if you have a friend with a truck who works for pizza or not.
- Background/Credit check $50-100
- Miscellaneous $200 – utility deposits, starter supplies
- Last month's rent $1000 (sometimes required)

You bring a couch and he brings his video gaming system and an extensive game library. He also brings his bulldog, Gumbo. You are probably more excited about living with Gumbo than Steve, because you love animals. This is going to be great!

But wait. Where is the Wi-Fi? Where is the cable? Where are the LIGHTS?

Oh, yeah. Utilities have to be set up. And before you get too deep into this roommate thing, some important decisions have to be made about bills. The smartest way to do this is an upfront roommate contract so that everyone has a clear understanding of who is paying what, when, and how.

Splitting Utilities

Before you start splitting up costs and responsibilities, you need to know what bills you will have each month. Some common household bills to keep in mind include:

- Rent
- Electricity
- Water
- Gas (when applicable)
- Sewer and Trash
- Cable or Satellite
- Internet
- House Phone (when applicable)
- Household supplies (Cleaning, bathroom, etc.)

Some of these will be a constant amount, others will vary based on usage. Many times you can get an average of what the last tenant paid each month, just for a ballpark idea of your monthly costs.

There are plenty of ways to go about paying your bills with roommates, but a lot of them lead to trouble. If someone doesn't pay a certain bill on time, that puts everyone else in jeopardy of losing the service. The best option to prevent issues is to use auto-draft from a joint savings account.

1. Set up a joint savings account for you and Steve for household expenses. If you do not trust each other well enough to know that no one will take money from the account, you can set it up so that both of you have to be present to authorize a withdrawal.

2. Create an automatic draft from each of your personal bank accounts to deposit money into the joint account each month. If Steve needs to see the bill first, he can wait to view it and then transfer the money in the joint bill account.

3. Set up another auto draft, but this time make it go from the joint account to each of the bill companies you have to pay. This way, you won't have to worry about making sure the bills get paid on time. They will automatically be paid for you, as long as you all maintain your contributions to the account.

4. Check your monthly bills to make sure there aren't any charges that exceed what you have put away. If so, make sure you all discuss those charges as a group and put the right amount of money into the account.

5. If there is extra money in the account, let it ride. Leave it in there to cover possible overages in the future. If you have money left at the end of your lease, you can split it up amongst yourselves.

There are risks in this setup, the largest being if one person doesn't have enough money in his or her personal account to transfer into the joint account to cover the bills. However, this is the most hassle-free way to split expenses.

If you take a different approach and you pay the bills and Steve pays you his share, don't forget or be shy about demanding prompt payments from your roommate every month. Even if you're only paying $50 in utilities a month, don't let it add up until the end of the year, or Steve may disappear from your life without squaring up.

Creating a Contract

It's really easy NOT to make these decisions. It seems like a bother and both you and Steve have the best of intentions to be fair to one another. You must capitalize on these good feelings to create a roommate contract early on. Clear, up-front communication will save a lot of grief later. Once you start getting irritated with Steve's habit of leaving your towel on the bathroom floor in a wet heap, you won't be in the mood to bargain over his heat bill – What the hell, Steve, it's like a sauna in your room!

SAVE TIME AND EFFORT LATER BY TALKING NOW!

And don't just talk, WRITE YOUR AGREEMENTS DOWN. This will be your contract, even if it's on a piece of torn scratch paper. A clear agreement will keep the peace most of the time, but also give you a leg to stand on if you and Steve decide you hate each other and end up in small claims court.

Here is a checklist of things to discuss with Steve.

- What is each person paying in rent? When is it paid? What is the penalty for being late?

- Document your utility payment agreement and the method they will be paid.

- Deposit – you put a significant damage deposit down. But what if Steve and Gumbo incur all the damage? Make an agreement about how to split any damage refund, or that it will be his sole responsibility if Gumbo goes all ragin' Cajun on the carpets. Walk the apartment and take pictures of any pre-existing damage to make sure you don't get charged for it upon move out. If there is a specific and additional pet deposit, Steve should be the one to pay it, regardless of how much you love Gumbo

- Guests – is it okay for Steve to have overnight guests? What about for a week at a time? What about his new girlfriend that spends most nights? Does he become responsible for more rent if he has another person staying in his room? What about YOU? Can your cousin Larry crash on your couch when he is in town? Maybe Steve hates strangers sleeping in his living room. It's a good time to find out expectations. This is a common issue that causes friction among roommates.

- Groceries – how will you split food? Will you buy your own? What is the policy on eating one another's left overs? What about the pantry items Steve's mom drops off every week – can you eat those or are they just for Steve and Gumbo? If Steve is proud of his hot sauce collection, you may want to consider labeling things kept in the 'fridge to avoid accidentally using the last of his rooster sauce and catching hell from a hangry gamer.

- Chores – what are the expectation around cleanliness? You don't have to fill out a chore board like mom did, but at least talk about the level of clean you want for your place. If you like a clean house but don't like to clean yourself, better lower your expectations for your roommate. Doing someone else's dishes sucks and people quickly grow to resent it. Steve will throw your fluffy laundry into a basket where it will get all wrinkly and require ironing. Unless you are quick with your folding game, then Steve won't have to do that. You and Steve can stay friends.

- Decide what you will do if you or Steve decide to move out before the end of the six-month lease. Will the person who has moved out be responsible for paying the full amount for all months still on the lease? Or will the person who stays behind agree to find a new roommate ASAP to avoid this situation? Anyone who signed the lease is legally responsible. Real talk. Stuff happens in life and best to have a plan.

Whoop – Agreement made! You both sign it and file a copy so that you can refer back to it. But you won't need to. You and Steve are going to get along forever! You order a single-topping celebratory pizza which you pay for equally.

Now stick to the agreement

Shoot. It's the first month and Steve hasn't given you his half of the power bill yet. It is due tomorrow. Your instinct is to be passive aggressive because you are not used to confronting people about household issues. You want to call your dad and complain, or a sympathetic friend, but instead you adult-up, grab the agreement, and knock on his bedroom door. Don't get mad (yet), without talking to Steve and trying to resolve the situation.

You show Steve the bill and firmly request he consult the agreement where he agreed to pay by the 5th of each month. He says he doesn't have the money right now. Gumbo had to visit the vet and needed some shots. You are fair and understanding, but also remind him that you work at the same crappy place and don't have any extra money either. He is responsible for his portion and you need it tonight to pay the bill on time and not incur a late fee. Steve has to borrow $60 from his mom to deposit into your joint account. That's fine. You stuck to your guns and had a talk with your roommate, good job. Because you were assertive and communicated openly, he may just remember to pay on time next month. At the very least he will know you are serious about sticking to the agreement.

Breaking a Lease

It's not working out with Steve. It's been four months and your soul is withering from the constant din of techno music coming from his room. You hate his food smells, you hate his black light, and you REALLY hate his new girlfriend. The agreement you made early on says that she can only stay over a few nights a week, so Steve now spends a good amount of time at her place across town, which is perfectly fine with you. Until a week goes by and you don't see or smell him. You get suspicious. You look in his room and see he has taken his gaming system. He's already gone…leaving you alone in the apartment with nothing but the lingering smell of Gumbo.

Just as you feared, Steve doesn't bother to pay rent that month. The landlord leaves a note on your door telling you to pay within 5 days or move out.

Move out, you think, that is an option!

Well, it would be if you hadn't signed a six month lease. You have two months to go. Moving out now will damage your credit – and as you currently have almost no other credit, that is a bad thing. (See, *Why you should care about your credit score , page 5.*)

Moving out early would accomplish nothing because you are on the hook to pay the rent for the entire term of the lease whether you live there or not. A landlord inviting you to move out if you cannot pay is not absolving you of responsibility for the lease unless they specifically say so in writing.

Happily, Steve is also on the lease, so this problem is his as well. You call him and remind him that, if he doesn't pay the rent, both of you will suffer the wrath of the credit gods. He doesn't care. He is in love and also broke.

Here is where you might have to get creative. In order to pre-serve your credit you MIGHT have to pay Steve's portion of the rent up front (somehow) and then sue him later to recoup it. Your property manager probably won't just take your half of the rent and call him delinquent on his part – you are all one renter to them. However it is worth your time to call and talk about it. Tell them Steve left you in a lurch and you are doing your best to figure out how to make it right. Who knows, they may offer you some kind of solution, or at least understanding. However, don't depend on that. Instead go under the assumption that you have to pay, and pay on time, to avoid big fees and credit damage. Many rental places charge up to $50 a day for late rent, so pay as quickly as possible.

If you can't shoulder the rent on your own and your family isn't able to help, you may need a temporary roommate. Ask around, look for someone you know. If you do take to the internet to find someone, make sure to vet them thoroughly and be safe, though you don't have to be told THAT after what happened with STEVE.

You manage to pay the rent, but now Steve owes YOU his half for the months he didn't pay. If you get the damage deposit back, you may be able to keep his portion against the debt he owes. He may also owe you for utilities based on the agreement and what-ever was outstanding when he left.

Moving out the legit way

You meet Becky. Becky is perfect. Becky CLEANS. Becky has respect for your dishwasher loading technique. She is everything Steve is not. Becky is a CAT PERSON. You decide to become roomies. The two of you make plans to rent a little house across town. Everything will be PERFECT.

When you move out, notify the landlord well in advance. Your rental lease may stipulate 30 days, that's pretty common. Give them your plans in writing. Find out what you have to do to re-ceive your deposit back and tell them you'd like your last month's rent applied (whoo hoo, you forgot for a while that Steve already had chipped in his half for the last month).

CLEAN YOUR HOUSE – if you don't, there will be a clean-ing fee. Clean it really well. Like, inside the oven and vacuum the closets. Anything you don't do will be billed back to you. It's easier to just do it. Ask your clean freak aunt to help, she loves wiping down cupboards.

Take pictures of damage – anything that looks different from when you moved in. Keep them on file, you may need them later if the rental company exaggerates the damage. Rental disputes are generally settled based on who has the most documentation to substantiate their claims.

Immediately discontinue your utilities. If you put it off, some nice couple that moves in behind you will have some awesome free cable, while you pay additional months. Be proactive, make the calls! Switch your service to your new address with Becky and get ready to start living the dream!

Right after she agrees to the contract terms.

How to deal with a situation in which you have broken/stained/ ruined someone else's property

We've all been there. You are standing in the foyer of someone's home and you gesture wildly and knock over an antique vase or sculpture...

No? You've never been there? Okay how about THIS:

You're sitting at a coffee shop with a couple of friends, working on a project of some kind. You gesture wildly and knock a full, burning hot, 20 ounce caramel latte all over the table which is occupied mostly by the MacBook Air which belongs to the person at the table you know the least. Sparks fly. The screen goes black.

Or what about this: You're drinking a red Gatorade and you trip and spill it all over your friend's white couch (I KNOW! What kind of a person gets a WHITE COUCH??).

OH, oh, this one is good! You borrow your friend's car to go to work and it gets broken into and the stereo stolen or maybe you get rear-ended (through ABSOLUTELY no fault of your own) and a fair amount of damage is done to the vehicle.

While you may want to run away, or sink into the earth or strategically place an afghan on the couch to cover the stain because no one saw you spill it, this is not the answer. The first step is to take a deep breath, admit the issue, and apologize.

There are a few reactions you might get, depending on the personality of the person whose property you have damaged:

- The person who wants everyone to be happy and will pretend that it isn't a big deal, even though it may be a really big deal.

- The person who EXPLODES at you and calls you all sorts of names and basically accuses you of being a worthless waste of space in the universe because you tripped over a cord (THEIR CORD) that was stretching across their living room and spilled on their stupid white couch.

- The person who immediately gets into the dollars and cents of the situation spouting things like, "WHO is going to pay for this? Yes I DO have insurance but I have no intention of using it because my rates will go up!"

So, we've covered that you need to apologize, and if you are faced with the person who is berating you as a human being for an honest mistake, it can be hard to remain calm. Responding with something like, "I can see that you are very angry and upset and I am extremely sorry for this accident. I will work with you to find a solution, but I'm going to ask you to stop attacking me, because it was an accident and I don't deserve the things you are saying." If they keep going, feel free to leave and let them know that you will contact them tomorrow when hopefully they have calmed down and you can have a respectful conversation. Keep in mind, this reaction is not super common, though it may be the worst case scenario which leaps into your mind first.

To the person who insists that it is nothing and you shouldn't give it a second thought, I'd suggest something like this, "You are being so gracious about this, but I do want to offer my help in some way. Please, let me help fix it/look for a replacement/clean up this mess."

Now. If you have spilled something (a gallon of paint, a glass of red wine), work quickly. Ask for some paper towels, some rags and two buckets or large bowls, one with water in it. Sop up as much as you can with the paper towels and then go to work with wet rags. You would not believe how much magic water and rags can do if applied promptly and vigorously. Carbonated water may help lift a stain. Rent a steam cleaner if you have to. Do your best. It is not reasonable for you to be expected to buy a new $2,000 couch for your friend. I'd say the most that you should do is the cleaning and possibly pay for a professional to give it a go if you can't erase the stain.

If you have insurance, and the item that has been damaged or destroyed has significant financial value, you could call your renter's insurance or car insurance agent as is appropriate and ask if it might possibly be covered. You might also suggest that your friend/acquaintance do the same with THEIR insurance companies and then you can discuss the options.

A little known benefit of many credit cards is something called "purchase protection." Your friend who just bought the couch or the MacBook Air with their credit card should absolutely call the credit card company and ask if their card has purchase protection for this item. The credit card company might pay for a new one. Seriously. This is a thing. It isn't on all cards—not debit cards usually, and typically on the type of credit cards that have some sort of "rewards" associated, but it is worth calling and asking. Of course there are all sorts of restrictions and loopholes, but it's worth checking!

Some things you can't make right. Accidents happen. Maybe you hit someone's cat with your car and kill it. This is horrible, and chances are, there isn't anything you could have done. The best you can do is take responsibility, apologize, and maybe make them a card expressing your regrets. Do not buy them a new cat.

Seriously. If the animal is injured but not killed, and if you can afford it, contributing to the veterinary costs is a nice gesture, but just do what you can.

The bottom line is that things get broken and ruined sometimes. You trip and break the urn containing the ashes of great aunt Sara sometimes. If you are the type to immediately go to the "it's not my fault" place, maybe take some responsibility. If you are the type to land in the "I AM A HORRIBLE HUMAN BEING AND DON'T DESERVE TO LIVE" place, please, take it easy on yourself. Everyone has a story (or 20) about the time they screwed up or tripped or ruined something. It's okay. We are human. Be brave, be honest, and be kind. Everyone will survive this.

Decision Tree:
Should you call in sick today?

ARE YOU ACTUALLY SICK?
PART 1

YES

Are you injured or in unusual physical pain?

Yes
Is the pain new or much worse?

Yes
STAY HOME. Consider seeing a doctor

No
Pain is ongoing from a known condition (ie cramps or a headache). Medicate, hydrate, and try to **GO TO WORK**

Are you contagious?

Yes
If you are in the first days of the flu or a severe cold, **STAY HOME** for the good of all

No
Could you have seasonal allergies or a hangover? If so, hydrate, medicate and **GO TO WORK**, knuckle-head

---

Do you need to stay near a bathroom?

Yes
If you need to stay near a bathroom for the foreseeable future, **STAY HOME** because, yuck

ARE YOU ACTUALLY SICK?
PART 2

NO, BUT...

Family Emergency

Sick Kid

If your kid is sick and you can't find a trusted person to watch them **STAY HOME**

Death in the Family

If a CLOSE family member has just died, you may **STAY HOME** to grieve.

DO NOT LIE ABOUT THIS. It will destroy trust.

Job Interview or Doctor Appointment

Improving your situation is a legit reason to miss work. Try to make plans to be absent ahead of time, but **STAY HOME** or try working a half day

Severe Weather

Depends on the expectations of your workplace. Generally, if you CAN make it safely to work, **GO TO WORK**

Household Emergency

If your water heater or septic tank has exploded, you may need to **STAY HOME** and deal. However, if waiting will not cause more damage, **GO TO WORK**

Mental Health Day

Depends. Can you take an unplanned day off without causing chaos at your work? Has it been a looooong time since you last called in? Be careful with this one and DO NOT post about your day's fun on Facebook, knucklehead

Employers do not like employees who are constantly calling in sick. Limit your call-ins to situations that really require it. However, if you are waking up every morning dreading work, it may be time to put your energy into finding a job that is better suited to you.

Tip for calling in: Keep it GENERAL. Do not go into detail about your illness or situation. As long as you are using good judgement and miss work infrequently, your boss should respect your privacy. If you are out of sick or vacation time, avoid calling in unless circumstances are truly dire. Many people lose their jobs for excessive absenteeism, or are passed over for promotion.

What to do if someone asks you to bail them out of jail

This one sucks. You are going along with your day when you get a collect call from the local jail. It is a friend or family member calling to say that they have been arrested and would you please, please bail them out because you are the only friend or family member who is cool enough to help and nobody else really cares about them and dear god, they can't spend another night in jail. PLEASE.

First, jail is really demoralizing and sad. Your friend or family member is probably not exaggerating how horrible it is and how much they don't want to be there. Compassion is a totally appropriate response here, even if the friend/family member was being a dumbass and doing something stupid like vandalizing a school when they got arrested. However, you can be compassionate and still not bail them out. Remember that as you go through this process.

Bailing someone out of jail is a big deal.

Let's say someone has a $5,000 bail/bond. First you need to find out if it is a cash bond, meaning you pay the whole amount in cash to the court/jail/booking officer or if it could be paid with a bail bond service, where you come up with 10-20% (usually) of the bond in cash or clear title of a car or something, and the bondsman (or bondswoman) pays the rest, but YOU are on the hook if your friend doesn't show up for all of their court dates, hearings, etc.

Scenario 1: Cash Bail of $5,000. Let's imagine you have the money. You will pay the bond and take responsibility for the arrested person.

- If they screw up in any way, you will probably not get your money back. Ever.

- If they are really good and go to all of their court dates, eventually the situation will resolve in an acquittal or conviction. You should get all of your money back within 6 weeks of the conclusion of the case. Be sure to get the case number and all relevant information in case you need to chase down your money.

Scenario 2: Bail Bond of $5,000. You find a bail bondsman who will offer to pay $4,000 of the bond if you pay $1,000 (20% in this scenario. Sometimes 10% will do it) AND if you convince them that your friend or family member is a low risk and is unlikely to jump bail or screw up in any other way. Here is the important thing – you have to have something of value (a car with clear title, or something similarly valuable) that you put up as collateral.

- If your friend or family member doesn't show up for their court dates, the bail bondsman/woman will lose the $4,000 they put up and will come after you for restitution (probably with some fee on top of the $4000) and you forfeit the $1,000 you originally put up

- If your friend or family member DOES show up for the court dates, you will still probably never see your money again because the bail bondsman will charge you 10-20% of the total bail as their fee.

So. Now you need to decide whether or not you should do it. Maybe the money for a cash bond can be raised by asking mutual friends to contribute money, but someone (you) still will have to take responsibility for the person when they are bailed out.

If this person is your brother or sister or parent, then you know them pretty well and can assess the risk of them freaking out once they are bailed out, or going on a drug/alcohol bender and not showing up for court. Assuming they are not battling addiction, and just made a stupid choice this one time, you may decide to do it.

Your best friend or boyfriend/girlfriend needs to be evaluated by the same criteria, but you also have to ask why their parents/siblings aren't bailing them out. Do they know something you don't?

If the person asking to be bailed out is someone that you were once close with but you've drifted apart, you really need to think hard. People can change quickly in these years of life and you don't know if the person who was your best friend sophomore year in Honors English is in a downward spiral and started doing meth last spring because you haven't talked to them in a year.

Look at the charges too. Drug charges (of a hard variety) can indicate addiction and even your best friend might screw you over if they are secretly addicted to heroin because that is what heroin does. Ask your friend/family member if they did what they are charged with, and why. If they have elaborate excuses about how it isn't their fault and they aren't to blame AT ALL, you have to decide whether you believe them or not. We all know of cases where someone was pulled over by a cop for a superficial reason and the things escalated unreasonably. But most of the time, if someone gets arrested, there is some reason for it, though often they get charged with the largest possible set of charges which might be unreasonable and the charges will eventually be reduced. If your friend can't take any responsibility for their part in the situation, they may not take responsibility for the consequences and might not show up for court.

You shouldn't bail someone out if losing that money will cost you dearly, like you won't be able to pay college tuition next quarter or make rent next month. (See, **What to do when a friends asks to borrow money, page 9.**) Assume you will not get your money back (and if you use a bail bondsman, you probably will not). If you can't afford to lose that money, you probably can't afford to bail someone out of jail.

You CAN be compassionate. You can try to gather support or find someone else who may be able to help. You can find out how to visit or have phone calls with your friend so they know you are thinking of them and care about them. You can keep track of their case and show up for moral support at their court dates. You can reach out to their lawyer to better understand what is happening and how to help. These are all really great ways to support someone in jail and they are things that most people won't do.

Be kind. Be wise. If you can also be generous, and it feels like something that would be both kind and wise, then do it. If generosity would be kind but stupid, don't do it.

Learn useful skills
Like how to change a tire

Picture this – you and three friends go for a day trip to the mountains. You friend has borrowed his Dad's old Toyota 4 Runner and you're going to do some light off-roading. Then the vehicle gets a flat tire. Your friend says, "Dude, that sucks, but I'm on my parent's AAA policy. No worries."

Except there is no reception on the mountain. Your friend can't call AAA. Worries ensue. Everyone starts remembering movies about friends trapped on a mountain involving frostbite and cannibalism. Everyone is about to freak out when you casually say, "I know how to change a tire. We'll be back on the road in 15 minutes."

The day is saved! YOU are the superhero!

Some tips:

- Always check to make sure you have a spare tire and a jack and ideally, the owner's manual for the car. Many new cars are being sold without a spare to reduce overall weight of the vehicle and subsequently, the gas efficiency they can claim for the car. This is stupid. Get a spare tire if your car doesn't have one and check it periodically to make sure it has enough air pressure.

- If you are on the freeway and get a flat, it typically will happen in two ways

  » You have a leak which results in low pressure which you may not have noticed until suddenly it feels like the road is really messed up. The tread may start to come off the tire and you will hear a "thu-thunk, thu-thunk, thu-thunk" sound and you might think you ran over something and are dragging it. Pull over as soon as possible.

> » Your tire blows out with a sudden loss of pressure. The sound is loud, and the car will jerk dramatically. It is up to you to keep control. Do not panic. Do not slam on the brakes. Try to maintain speed until you have clearance to pull over. Do this as soon as possible, and be sure to get well out of the road when you do it. Give yourself a second to let your heart return to normal and then give yourself a pat on the back for being a badass who managed a blow out on the freeway with nobody getting hurt. And now promote yourself to super badass and change that tire.

- DO NOT DRIVE ON A FLAT. If you have a standard compact car, you can probably replace your tire for around $60. If you drive on the flat tire for too long, the rim will get damaged. Now you have to replace that. If you have a bigger car and you drove on the flat for a long time, you may have messed up way more than just the rim and it could cost hundreds of dollars (even thousands if you're driving a super fancy pants car).

- Have a tire pressure gauge in the glove box and know how to use it and read it. If a tire looks low, check it. It will take you about 2 minutes and is totally worth it. Throw a package of wet wipes in the glove box while you are at it. Tires are dirty and you will want to clean your hands up a bit.

Now you know WHY you should know how to change a tire. It is time to understand HOW. First, let me say that this is a skill best learned by doing, alongside someone who is experienced. Set aside a morning with someone car-smart and have them spot you while you practice and get tips from them.

CHANGING A TIRE

1. Find a flat, firm piece of ground on which to change the tire. Not squishy, deep mud, not quicksand. DO NOT change a tire on an incline.

2. Put the car in park (or 1st gear for a stick) and put on the e-brake. Obviously, turn the car off (that is obvious, right?)

3. Gather up what you need and get it out of the car.

4. BEFORE you jack the car up, loosen (but DO NOT REMOVE) the lug nuts of the affected tire. If you don't see the lug nuts, you may need to remove a hubcap which is covering them.

   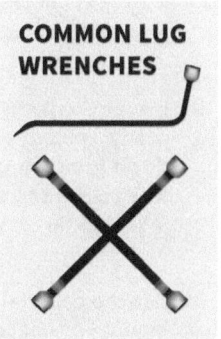

   COMMON LUG WRENCHES

   It can be really hard to get them loose. You can use your foot to help, but don't jump on it. You can mess up the car and yourself that way. To loosen, you turn them to the left (or counter-clockwise). One rotation of loosening is usually sufficient. If you have a pipe in the trunk (you MIGHT!), you can put it on the wrench (they call this a "cheater bar") which gives you more leverage and makes it easier.

5. If you have a block (wood or a rock or something), put it in front of one of the non-affected tires to add extra assurance that the car won't roll. If it is your passenger side rear tire that is flat, put the block in front of the driver side front tire.

6. Now, put the jack in the right spot. The right spot should be specified in the owner's manual or even on the jack sometimes. If you can't find that information, put it under the strongest part of the frame – it should be part of the main frame and is usually 6-12 inches from the wheel.

7. Jack it up! Don't get frustrated. If this is your first time, you may reach a point of anxiety where your brain says "THIS IS STUPID AND IMPOSSIBLE AND THIS JACK MAKES NO SENSE!!!" If that happens, take a deep breath. You can do this.

8. Once the car is jacked up, remove the lug nuts completely (put them somewhere they won't roll away), take off the flat and put the spare on. You might find that you need to jack the car up one or two more pumps to give yourself extra room. This can be tricky because it is like threading 4-6 big needles at the same time. If someone is with you, this is a good time to get help, as it is easier with two people.

FIVE-LUG

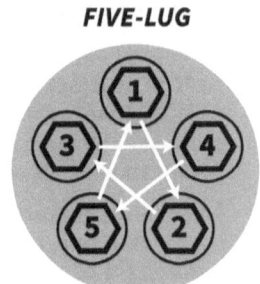

9. Put the lug nuts on but don't tighten them super tight yet. You want to tighten them in a way that gets the tire snugged up evenly around the whole thing. Like so:

10. Lower the jack, then make sure the lugs are really as tight as you can make them (again, don't jump on the lug wrench). You've done it! Pack up the wrench and the flat and the jack and be on your way!

11. Get the original tire repaired or replaced within a week. The spare tire may be a "space saver" and is really just meant for emergencies. Don't drive on it for long.

How to not get fired because of what you post online

The internet has been around long enough for all of us to have seen good behavior and bad behavior on public display. Now, I can't really tell you how to be. You have your own identity. Maybe you're into showcasing your abs, your inner party animal, or your fringy views on politics. Maybe you revel in terrible puns. You may behave in a way that 98% of your friends and followers find charming. But when it's time to get a job or move up the ladder, your public persona can really hold you back.

Here are some quick tips on controlling your social media presence without totally changing for the man.

- Protect your Facebook profile so only friends can view it. It's extremely common for HR departments and independent employers to look you up online before extending an offer. Do not let prospective employers cruise your spring break pictures. Even though you look smoking hot in your swim suit, beer pong champion may not be the qualification HR is looking for.

- Even better, change your profile name slightly so that it doesn't match the name on your resume. People will not be able to find you unless you give them the unique spelling.

- If you want to be really tricky, make a second, very proper profile under your full name. If you don't mind leading a bit of a double life, this is a great solution to put your best foot forward.

- Do not, DO NOT friend co-workers/bosses/clients/anyone from HR. Tell people outright that you like to keep your work life and personal life separate, and so they should not be upset if you don't accept their friend request. If they grow into a really good friend? Well, okay, it happens. But now you must always remain aware that someone linked to your workplace has a view into your weekends – beware. A picture of you at the beach posted on the day you called in sick is suddenly fodder for work gossip.

- Do not post about your workplace, or anything that happens there. It is bad manners to cast your employer in a negative light. Even if they are jackasses, even if a customer was a total douche canoe to you, even if your boss has his zipper down at the big meeting – SAY NOTHING. Bite your lip, save the juicy story for in- person conversations. If you put your complaints on the internet, they inevitably are read by people you did not intend to see them. Or, a year later, a prospective employer could just notice that you seem to display poor judgement and a lack of loyalty. It's okay to say positive things, but keep it general and above board. Example: Okay to say "I love my job!" not okay to say, "I love my job, all the free ice cream I can eat!" A carefree statement from you can be interpreted as unethical behavior by others.

- Understand the repercussions of posting anything that involves other people. Ask permission, always. It may put people into an awkward position for a variety of reasons, always be sensitive to the way others want to be represented on the internet.

So, be yourself. But be smart about with whom you share your real self on the internet. Let your employer judge you by the merits of your work, not by the number of times you used the F-bomb as your March madness bracket collapsed.

What to do if your credit or debit card is declined

You're at dinner with friends, or buying groceries or new shoes and when it is time to pay, your credit card or debit card is declined. What do you do?

A. Yell at the waiter/waitress/cashier/salesperson that you have plenty of money and obviously there is something wrong with "their system!"

B. Crawl under the table or rack of shoes or grocery cart in mortification

C. Panic and start digging through your wallet mumbling, "uhhh, I think I have…uhhhh…there HAS to be something…." and spread out loyalty punch cards and old receipts and raffle ticket stubs on the counter or table.

D. Calmly say, "That's strange, but you know how it is--my bank is so cautious, they probably just want to make sure it is me making the purchase. Can you give me a moment to sort this out?"

The answer is D! The clerk/waitress/cashier is JUST as uncomfortable as you are. They probably make slightly more than minimum wage themselves and have been in this situation. Now, here are the common reasons your card might be declined:

1. You don't have enough money in your debit card or enough available balance on your credit card.

a. This can happen for a variety of reasons aside from the obvious. Sometimes when you make a purchase the merchant authorizes or holds a larger amount than what you will actually be charged and it can take a few days for that hold to come off. This is NOTORIUSLY TRUE with gas stations. They will authorize up to $75 when you swipe your card at the pump and that amount will continue to be held for a couple of days (depending on your bank) even if you actually only put $20 of gas in your tank. It can also take a couple of days for funds to be available from a deposited check or for a refund to be processed. Be aware of this when you plan how much money you have available.

2. There is a security hold on your account

   a. Maybe you just bought a plane ticket or concert tickets online and now you are spending more money and it is unusual behavior on your account. Your credit card company has fraud prevention models to identify unusual activity and they will temporarily freeze your account until they can be sure it is you.

   b. Maybe your card has been compromised and a fraudster has been running up charges on your account.

3. Your payment was late and hasn't been processed yet

Just stay cool and call the number on the back of the card, speak (politely and respectfully) to the customer service person who answers (eventually—it can be a maze to get to a live person) and find out what is up and why the authorization was declined. Maybe it can be rectified over the phone. Maybe not. If you have eaten the food you are being charged for, or really need those groceries, this might be a good time to pull out your emergency credit card (you know, the one that you have for REAL EMERGENCIES) and use it instead. Buying shoes is not an emergency. If you are buying shoes in this scenario, ask the clerk if they can hold them for you for a day or two while your sort out some confusion at the bank.

If you don't HAVE an emergency credit card (which is wise, if you can't trust yourself to not buy shoes with it), then tell the grocery clerk that you are sorry, but there has been a mix up at the bank and you aren't able to sort it out right now. There are people whose job it is to put groceries back. Hold your head up and be polite and leave. Nobody cares, nobody will remember. If you throw a fit, people WILL care AND remember.

If you don't have an emergency credit card and you have just eaten the food you are supposed to pay for (i.e., you are at a restaurant), ask the server if you can speak with them privately and explain the situation. Apologize for the inconvenience to them and assure them that you DO intend to pay as soon as this is sorted out and ask what options there are. They may actually want you to wash dishes to work off the bill, but I have never heard of that really happening except on sitcoms. It is more likely that they will take your name and number and address and let you go. BE SURE TO RETURN AND PAY as soon as you can. You do not want bad restaurant karma.

Places to invite a date
when you are broke

Broke dates can be the best: the most romantic, the most adventurous, and the most memorable. You don't need a fancy waiter interrupting your seduction, or a boring movie smothering lively conversation. There is a ton of fun to be had for little or no money. Here are some suggestions for dating on the cheap:

- Outdoor movies – many neighborhoods have outdoor movie nights in the park or projected onto the back of the 7-11. Use the internet to track down one playing a movie your date might remember from a slumber party in their youth.

- Star gazing – check earthsky.org for a list of upcoming meteor showers. Then find a clearing away from city lights and wait quietly for someone to make the first move.

- Art museums – most admission prices are "suggested donation" and/or are free one night a month.

- A Japanese or Botanical garden in your city – every city has its hidden gems.

- Go on a night walk! Explore a neighborhood by night.

- Christmas lights! If it happens to be December, take your date to one of those neighborhoods that go Christmas bonkers. Bring a thermos of hot chocolate and pray for a dusting of romantic snow.

- Rainy day picnic – Pack some PB&Js and go to a park with a large picnic structure. It will be deserted on a really rainy day, so you'll need to run from the car to the shelter. Once you get underneath, with the rain thrumming down and creating a curtain between you and the world…I think you'll find the date is going well.

- Poetry Slam open mic – no, you don't HAVE to participate. You can huddle together in a dark corner and either love it or love hating it together.

- Anywhere with a fire pit – beach, woods, backyard, a fire pit always breeds intimate conversation.

- Bank heist – it's exciting AND you are no longer broke.

- Fly a kite – bonus points if you make the kite.

- Hike up something for a picnic with a killer view.

Learn useful skills
Like how to jump a car battery

You've been at a friend's house or a movie and walk to your car, get in, turn the key and nothing happens. Weird. Maybe you will hear a clicking noise, or maybe there is no sound at all.

First, make sure the car is in park (if it is an automatic). If for some reason it is in drive or reverse or something, the car will not start. Fix that and try again.

If it still won't start, you may have a dead battery. If you have an electric car, these instructions are not for you. These instructions are for someone with a standard gas or diesel powered car with an alternator and a battery. If you have this sort of car then you should have jumper cables. You should have long jumper cables. They should live in your trunk.

If you have AAA or some other roadside assistance, you can call them and they can come jump your car. If you don't, or if you don't have time to wait, you need to find someone with a car who is willing to jump you. Be polite, be apologetic, but don't be shy. Just walk up to the first non-ax-murder-y person you see and ask if they could please give you a jump. Maybe have the jumper cables in your hand so they know that you are a competent car owner and this will take just a moment of their time.

Open your hood and see which side of the car your battery is on. Have the other driver bring their car as close as possible (even so, you will see why you have the long cables). BOTH cars should be in park or neutral with the parking brake on and the engine turned off. I repeat—turn BOTH CARS OFF. Double check the dead car. The ignition should be in the off position.

Now, you need to CAREFULLY hook up the cables according to the following diagram and instructions. Take your time and make sure you have them attached correctly. This is very, very important.

1. Attach one of the red clips to the positive terminal of your battery. Look for the side that has "POS" or "+" on it (you may need to wipe off some grime to be able to see it). If you can't see a POS or + symbol, you may find that the positive terminal is bigger than the negative one.

2. Attach the other red clip on the other side of the cables to the positive terminal of the other car. Same instructions for finding it.

3. Attach one of the black clips to the negative terminal on the OTHER CAR'S battery.

The cables should look like this:

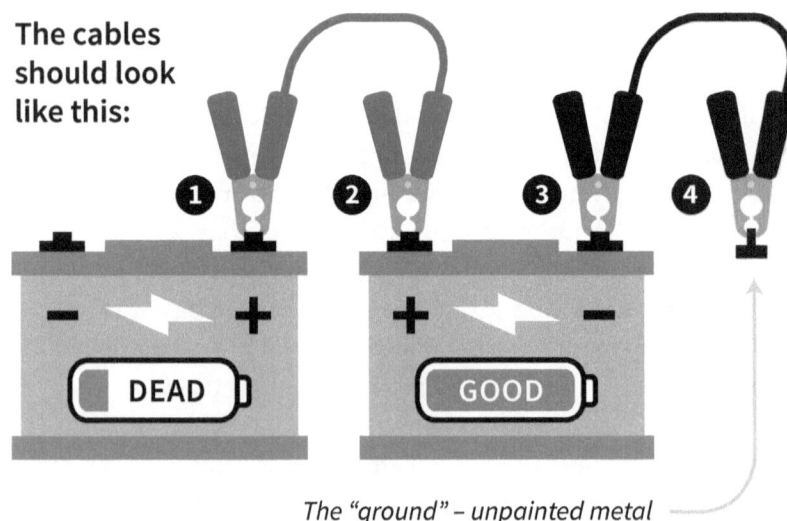

The "ground" – unpainted metal

4. Attach the last black clip to an unpainted metal surface on your car that isn't near the battery. This is the "ground" and it needs to be well attached. Take your time to get the ground right (again, you might need to clean some grime off). Sometimes the bar that lifts the hood up can work for this purpose.

5. Start the working vehicle (the other person's car) and let the engine run for a couple of minutes.

6. Now try to start your vehicle.

7. It starts! You can disconnect the cables, and wave goodbye to the other car after thanking the driver, **but don't turn your car off for at least a half an hour.** The running of the engine will finish charging up the battery. If you turn it off now, the battery won't have enough juice to start the car again. Give it some time.

   » If it won't start, make sure that the cables are properly connected and have the other person run their engine for a couple more minutes. You might ask them to increase the RPMs (put their foot on the gas a little bit). If it won't start after that, then I am afraid your battery is hosed and you will need to get a new one. You may now take back your cables (carefully) and thank the person who tried to help you. Call AAA now, or a friend or family member who can help you. Replacing a car battery isn't rocket science but it IS beyond the scope of this booklet.

   » If the car starts and you start driving and 5 minutes later the car dies and won't start again, your problem may be your alternator (which is the thing that converts the power of the engine into charge for the battery). If this is the case, then you have a problem that cannot be solved with a jump. You need a tow truck or a friend or family member who will spend an hour or two helping you limp your way to a mechanic one jump at a time.

Lawyers: When You Need Them, When You Don't
By: *An Actual, Practicing Lawyer*

Nobody likes lawyers. Shakespeare joked about killing them all in Henry VI, and our stock hasn't increased much in the intervening four hundred years. We are routinely denounced by politicians, celebrities, and talking heads on cable news. In media and literature we are often portrayed as scheming, mendacious psychopaths. Even my own family delights in relating jokes about lawyers that they wouldn't dream of saying about any other profession. (One example: What do you call a million dead lawyers? A good start!)

The good news: there are a lot of things involving the legal system that you can do on your own without hiring one of us scumbag lawyers.

The bad news: it is a near certainty that you will have to deal with a lawyer at some point in your life. The legal system in the U.S. is complex, and there are some aspects of it that are extremely difficult to navigate without some legal advice. Moreover, there will be times when consulting with a lawyer will save you a lot of time and money, or help keep you out of jail.

This article will provide some guidance about when you should consult with an attorney, and when you may be able to avoid paying attorney's fees.

Criminal Law

This one is simple. If you are being investigated for a crime or have been charged with a crime, you need to talk with a lawyer. Right now. "But, I'm innocent!" you say. It doesn't matter. I don't care if you have a pristine record, an ironclad alibi, and a character reference from the pope himself. Talk to a lawyer *before* you talk to the police.

Car Accidents and Personal Injury

Car accidents are by far the most common source of personal injury cases in the U.S. Insurance companies are usually involved in these cases, which creates a few complications. Here are a few basic rules to keep in mind:

- If you are involved in a car accident that resulted in injury (to you or to another person), you need to report the accident to your insurance company, as well as the police and/or DMV.

- If somebody files a lawsuit against you in connection with a car crash, you need to send a copy of the lawsuit to your own insurance company *right away*. In most cases, your insurance company will hire a lawyer to defend you at no cost to you.

- If you sustained an injury in a car crash that wasn't your fault, it is a good idea to consult with an attorney. Most personal injury attorneys don't charge for an initial consultations. Keep in mind that personal injury attorneys generally work on a contingency basis, which means they will keep a percentage (usually 25% to 40%) of whatever damages you recover.

- If you are having problems with your insurance company not paying a claim arising from a car accident, you generally have two options. One is to consult with an attorney, and the other is to file a written complaint with the agency that regulates insurance in your state.

If you are responsible for injuring another person outside of a car accident (say, for example, you accidentally maimed your neighbor with a weed whacker), you may be able to tender the claim under your homeowner's or renter's insurance policy, and have them hire a lawyer to defend you. By the same token, if you are injured by another person, you may be able to submit a claim to their insurance company. As with motor vehicle cases, you may be able to handle a smaller claim on your own, but there is relatively little downside to at least talking with a personal injury attorney about your claim, as most of them do not charge for initial consultations.

If you are injured on the job, your claim will generally be handled by a worker's compensation program that will pay your medical bills and a portion of lost income while you are recovering. If your worker's compensation claim is denied, or you are having problems collecting benefits, you probably need to talk with an attorney.

Family Law
Family law generally deals with issues of divorce and child custody (including adoption and surrogacy contracts). Whether you need a lawyer or not will depend on your specific circumstances. With divorce, many couples are able to separate amicably without hiring lawyers. Some couples agree to jointly pay for a mediator to resolve minor disputes rather than go to the expense of hiring lawyers and going to court. In general, if there are significant disagreements about child custody or spousal support, you should consult with a lawyer.

Estate Law and Real Property
150 years ago, each state had their own unique set of idiosyncratic laws, which meant that things like regulation of business contracts could vary considerably from state to state. Over time,

states have gradually brought commercial, criminal, and tort laws into alignment. In other words, while there are some minor regional variations, the basic principles of contracts, criminal law, and tort are pretty similar in every state.

Two areas where this alignment has *not* occurred are estate law (the law governing wills, probate, trusts, and other ways of passing assets after death) and real property law (the law governing ownership and transfer of land and buildings). While there isn't a lot of overlap between these two areas of the law, they both are governed by extremely complex rules that require rigid adherence to some bizarre and frequently outdated rules and regulations. Thus, these are two areas where it can be a ***really bad idea*** to rely on forms you downloaded off the internet.

Thankfully, if you are buying or selling land or buildings, real estate agents can handle the more arcane paperwork for you. If you are trying to handle a real estate transaction without an agent, you probably need to have a lawyer look at the paperwork to make sure it meets the legal requirements.

When it comes to preparing a will or setting up a trust, whether you need a lawyer or not will depend on what state you're in and what you're trying to do. As a rule of thumb, if you want your will to be enforceable, you should probably run it by a lawyer.

On the other hand, if a family member dies, it usually isn't necessary to hire a lawyer to administer their estate (a process referred to as "probate"). Probate courts are used to dealing with non-lawyers, and you can often find all of the forms and documents you need on the court's website. On the other hand, if the deceased person left a lot of assets, or if there is conflict among the heirs, the person administering should consult with an attorney about how to proceed.

Setting up A Business

If you want to start a new business, it is easy to set up and register a new limited liability company or corporation without a lawyer. In most states, the forms are available online, and take just a few minutes to fill out.

However, if your business involves more than one person, you should consult with a small business attorney. In any business that has more than one person, it is important to have a written agreement stating, for example, how decisions will be made, how profits and losses will be allocated, and how the business partners will handle internal disputes. In addition to drafting this agreement, a small business attorney can also help you obtain any necessary business licenses, insurance coverage, and other things your business will need.

Bankruptcy

If you are considering filing for bankruptcy, you should consult with an attorney. Many offer free initial consultations.

Some jurisdictions have recently developed special filing systems to help self-represented individuals file for chapter 7 bankruptcy. These are not available everywhere, and even in places where this is an option, it is still a good idea to consult with an attorney.

Small Claims

Small claims court is one area where you absolutely don't need a lawyer. In fact, in many places, you're not allowed to bring a lawyer to small claims court.

Small claims courts only handle small dollar disputes. What counts as a small dollar dispute changes from court to court, but small claims courts usually handle cases involving disputes of less than $10,000.

The rules of procedure in small claims tend to be extremely informal, and the process moves pretty quickly (it is not uncommon to get a trial date within a month or two of filing). Both sides bring their materials to court on their assigned day, and explain to the judge what happened and why they think they should prevail. The judge typically makes a ruling from the bench.

What kinds of disputes can you bring to small claims? Almost anything. Your neighbor knocked down your favorite tree, and refuses to pay for it? Your cable company kept charging you after you cancelled service, and won't issue a refund? Your landlord is dragging her feet on fixing the furnace in your apartment? The electronics store won't honor the extended warranty you bought for your TV? All of these things can be resolved in small claims court without having to hire a lawyer.

When in Doubt, Talk With a Lawyer

Perhaps you have a problem that isn't addressed above, and you're not sure whether you need a lawyer. Unfortunately, the best person to ask is a lawyer.

If you have a friend or family member with a law degree, give them a call and see if you can get some free basic legal advice (I field a few of these calls every month, many from Facebook friends I haven't spoken with since high school). If you don't know any lawyers, contact your state bar association. Most have a lawyer referral program that will put you in touch with a licensed attorney who offers initial consultations for free or at a nominal cost.

Should you get a dog?

Dogs. Are. The best. I can totally understand why you think you should get one. Have you been to the lake and seen the happy retrievers cavorting with a tennis ball? Or that little Teacup Yorkie your mom's friend kept in her purse? Who would not want a furry life companion like that for themselves? You can feel the hot doggie breath on your face already.

Wait. But do you have time for the dog? Not just time to walk it in the evening, but like TIME. What will the dog do during your work hours? Where will he go when you make spur of the moment weekend plans? You can figure it out, you say, you have roommates. Everyone will love your dog. Aw, he's going to be so cute, you might call him Marty.

Wait, how much is dogfood? Marty is pretty big. He's way bigger than they said he was going to be when you got him from the Humane Society. His shots cost a lot and he sometimes cries out in sharp pain – you are wondering if he's got stomach troubles from the cheap brand of dry food you switched him to. Or maybe it's something more serious. You hope you won't have to take him to the vet. You don't have the money to spend. You might be short on rent. That's okay, you needed a bigger yard for Marty, anyway.

But you won't be able to move easily, because once you have a doggie, you'll find rental options greatly diminished. People in apartments aren't too keen on dogs, especially when they are over 25 lbs. Your security deposit will double. You may never see the return of a damage deposit again.

So you'll get a house! You and a bunch of dog lovers will create a commune in which your dog is fully supported and fed organic turkey and fresh carrots twice daily between dips in the crick. If this is the case, GET A DOG RIGHT NOW (think about an old one, so many aging dogs are in need of a caring human).

However, if you work a lot, like to go out a lot, can't afford vet visits, or rent a small apartment, you should maybe pause and try to create a responsible situation to bring a dog into. Dogs become family and it's sad when humans adopt impulsively and then do not take care of them the way sweet, sensitive animals like dogs require.

You can still spoon cute dogs at the park. You can offer to dog-sit your friend's pit bull over Memorial Day, but try to look past your rampant desire for a canine companion and wait until the circumstances are right.

Same goes for babies.

How to make a hard decision

By now, you've probably already made some hard decisions. I wish I could tell you that decision making gets easier, but it doesn't. Mastering the art of it now instead of when you are 40 is a wise investment in your life. Every time you do it, you'll get better at it.

Here is what you do—narrow down your possible choices to two (or three or four if you are very ambitious or very confused) grab a stack of post-it notes and a sharpie. Write down one thing on every post it about the potential impact for each choice. Do it fast and don't edit or think too much. If I was trying to decide whether to change my college major from Poetry to Finance, I might write things like:

- Finance = money
- Money = security
- Poetry is my passion
- I want to show everyone I can be responsible
- I don't want to wear a suit
- Day traders can still write poetry
- My Dad thinks poetry is a ridiculous major
- I don't want to be a corporate sell out
- I don't want to be a starving artist
- I want to have a family one day and support them financially
- I want to have a family and teach them to follow their heart

They don't have to make SENSE. Two post-its can totally contradict each other. They can be childish and embarrassing and misspelled and make barely any sense. Nobody else has to see these. The point is to get ALL of the thoughts and fears and hopes surrounding the decision out of your head so you can really look at them. Now sort them on a big wall or table so they are all visible. In this example, I might create four quadrants like so:

	POETRY	**FINANCE**
PRO		
CON		

Every post-it note, every random thought, hope, fear, shred of anxiety needs to find a way into one of these quadrants. Then sit with it a minute. You may find that the "PRO" box for one side is bursting with post-its and the CON side for the other is bursting. Hooray! That's an easy one. Well…so it would seem. I might suggest in that scenario that you take a moment to ask yourself why you thought this decision would be hard. There is SOME reason, some person you were afraid of disappointing that made you afraid to decide. You should figure that out and address it, but your decision is clear.

Let's say it ISN'T so clear. Let's say there are plenty of PROs and CONs for each choice. Now what? Now comes round 2. Read all the CONs for one option and figure out the main themes. Maybe the "CON" quadrant for Poetry has 15 different versions of "You cannot make a living writing poetry." You can probably replace it with one post it that says that. Consolidate to the REAL issues for each quadrant.

Now for each of the CONS, try to make an argument to cancel it out. For "You cannot make a living making poetry" you might say, "I could teach poetry and make a modest income." If you feel good about that option, then maybe the money post it comes off the board. BUT if you immediately come up with a new CON saying, "I don't WANT to teach!! I want to write!" then post it comes back on.

This process should make the decision easier. If you still can't decide, then just pick one. Tell yourself (but no one else), "I CHOOSE FINANCE! I will change my major tomorrow!" (or buy a condo, or get married, or have a baby, or quit your job or move to Tallahassee or whatever your decision is about) and then go to sleep. In the morning, check in with how you feel about that decision. If you wake with a sense of excitement and peace, then you my friend, have made a good choice. If you wake up and want to cry or have a sick feeling in your stomach (one that feels like sadness and regret, not excitement), you probably didn't. Now say to yourself, "Screw this! I'm choosing poetry!" If you are flooded with a sense of relief and joy, then BING BANG BOOM. You've decided.

Also, give yourself a break. If you never make a mistake, you'll never learn anything. If you make the wrong decision, most of the time, the world won't end. Take a deep breath, be honest with yourself and kind to yourself. It's going to be okay.

www.ingramcontent.com/pod-product-compliance
Lightning Source LLC
Chambersburg PA
CBHW050509290526
45786CB00006B/2495